ELLIS ISLAND

ELLIS ISLAND
Coming to the Land of Liberty

RAYMOND BIAL

Houghton Mifflin Books for Children

HOUGHTON MIFFLIN HARCOURT

Boston • New York • 2009

Houghton Mifflin Books for Children
is an imprint of Houghton Mifflin Harcourt
Publishing Company.

www.hmhbooks.com

Book design by Lisa Diercks
The text of this book is set in Whitman.
Map by Jerry Malone

Library of Congress Cataloging-in-Publication Data
Bial, Raymond.
Ellis Island / Raymond Bial.
p. cm.
Includes bibliographical references.
ISBN 978-0-618-99943-9
1. Ellis Island Immigration Station (N.Y. and
N.J.)—History—Juvenile literature. 2. Ellis
Island (N.Y. and N.J.)—History—Juvenile
literature. 3. United States—Emigration
and immigration—History—Juvenile
literature. I. Title.
JV6484.B53 2009
304.8'73—dc22 2008036794

Printed in Singapore
TWP 10 9 8 7 6 5 4 3 2 1

Most of the images in this book were taken by
Raymond Bial at Ellis Island. The New York Public
Library also provided a number of historical
photographs from its impressive collections on
the following pages: 9, 12, 17, 24, 25, 28, 29, 31, 34,
35 (bottom), 39 (right), 40, and 41. Additionally,
Alfred Steiglitz's classic image *The Steerage* on
page 38 was provided courtesy of Art Resource
and Artists Rights Society (ARS), © 2008 Georgia
O'Keeffe Museum/Artists Rights Society, New York.

*I would like to thank the National Park Service for
permission to photograph at Ellis Island. I would
also like to thank our daughter Anna and her
husband, Jack, for shepherding us around New York,
our son, Luke, for lugging camera equipment, our
daughter Sarah for taking care of all our pets at
home while we were away, and my wife, Linda, for
always being there for me.*

—RAYMOND BIAL

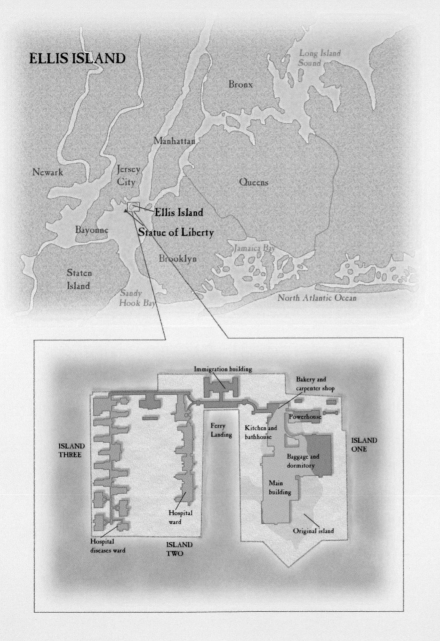

ELLIS ISLAND

Newark

Bronx

Long Island Sound

Manhattan

Jersey City

Queens

Bayonne

Ellis Island
Statue of Liberty

Staten Island

Brooklyn

Jamaica Bay

Sandy Hook Bay

North Atlantic Ocean

Immigration building

Bakery and carpenter shop

Ferry Landing

Kitchen and bathhouse

Powerhouse

ISLAND THREE

Baggage and dormitory

ISLAND ONE

Main building

Hospital ward

Original island

Hospital diseases ward

ISLAND TWO

This book is lovingly dedicated to my wife, Linda, our grandparents, and our children. Our grandparents came to America from many other countries: Germany, Hungary, Italy, Lithuania, Poland, and Slovenia. Like millions of other immigrants, they arrived at Ellis Island and other ports of entry and worked hard to make a home for their families in the land of liberty. To visit Ellis Island so many years later and walk in their footsteps for a few moments with Linda and our children was one of the most poignant experiences of my life.

Every year, more than two million people journey from their distant homes to visit Ellis Island, within the shadow of the Statue of Liberty. What are these visitors hoping to find on this small island, which was once a landfill in the upper bay of New York Harbor?

Since the first European explorers ventured to what would become known as North America, immigrants have been coming to the "New World" to escape political tyranny, religious intolerance, or poverty. These migrations continued from the founding of Jamestown in 1607 through the colonial era to 1776 when America declared its independence. Over the next 250 years to the present day, millions of people have made the long journey to the United States—the land of liberty. Waves of early immigrants, from 1820 to 1880, came largely from Western and Northern Europe: England, Ireland, Scotland, Wales, Germany, France, Belgium, Holland, Denmark, Norway, Sweden, and Switzerland. Many of

these newcomers faced discrimination, especially the Irish. Some Americans wanted to limit and even stop the flood of immigrants. However, other people believed that immigrants were, in the words of Abraham Lincoln, "a source of national wealth and strength."

Beginning in 1880, waves of immigrants, escaping from poverty, political oppression, and religious persecution, came increasingly from countries in eastern and southern Europe. Most of these immigrants came from Italy, Poland, Russia, and Austria. Many also came from Hungary, Bulgaria, Turkey, Serbia, and Montenegro, along with continuing emigration from Germany, Ireland, and England. Whatever their country of origin, all of these peoples longed for a better life in America. As one Italian immigrant stated, "If America did not exist, we would have had to invent it for the sake of our survival."

ABOVE: This Ellis Island display shows maps of the United States and Europe, including travel routes in the largest migration in human history.

PREVIOUS SPREAD: Every year more than two million people stroll through these doors at Ellis Island just as their ancestors did two, three, or four generations ago.

Many of these people were desperate to escape poverty and even starvation in their home countries. In Poland there was a saying that people journeyed to America for *za chlebem,* meaning "for bread." Another said that immigrants came "for bread, with butter." Charles Bartunek, who came from Czechoslovakia and settled in New York in 1914, explained, "We'd have meat about once a year . . . Once in a while, Mother would buy one of those short bolognas, cut it up, put it in a soup,

and everybody would get a little piece. I used to think, 'If [only] I could get enough of that to fill my stomach!' "

Other people had to flee for their lives. In March 1915, the Muslim Turkish government decided to rid their country of all Armenian Christians. Some were murdered in their homes at the hands of the Turks, and others died of thirst and hunger on a forced march through the desert. From 1915 to 1923 the Turkish government massacred as many as one and a half million Armenians. More than a half million Armenians escaped to America, and many of these refugees passed through Ellis Island.

In Russia, many Jews were robbed, beaten, and slaughtered in vicious attacks

Many immigrants, including Christians and Jews, fled from Europe to escape religious persecution.

called pogroms. "We had taken shelter in the attic of a house because a pogrom was raging in our town and we were hiding from the mob," Sophie Trupin recalled. "It was up in that attic, surrounded by his terrified family, that my father vowed that he would leave this accursed Russia and make a new life for himself and his family in America."

Since its opening on January 1, 1892, Ellis Island in New York Harbor has come to symbolize the waves of immigrants from these areas of Europe. Although there were more than seventy other federal immigration stations along the boundaries and shores of the United States, between 1892 and 1924, half of the newcomers to the United States passed through Ellis Island. The busiest year for the little island was 1907, when more than a million people came through this port of entry. Today, four of every ten Americans can trace their family history through Ellis Island. As they stroll about the grounds and view the exhibits, visitors gain an appreciation of what it was like to cross the Atlantic Ocean and make one's way through Ellis Island into an unknown country. While they are seeking their family roots, people can better understand the lives of their ancestors as newly arrived immigrants to the United States. In an age in which both the joys and the heartbreak of immigrants have often been forgotten, a visit to Ellis Island provides tender glimpses into the complex and touching experiences of immigrants who longed to find

Among the more powerful exhibits at Ellis Island are portraits of immigrants who made the long journey to the shores of America.

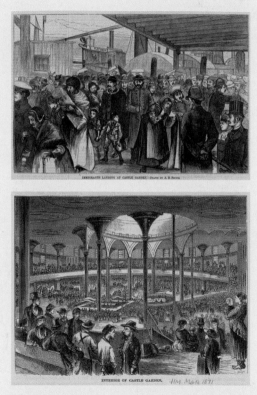

a home in a new land. Louis Sage, a fifteen-year-old who emigrated from Poland, recalled, "America was on everyone's lips. We talked about America; we dreamt about America. We all had one wish — to be in America."

There are countless stories of so many people who overcame seemingly insurmountable obstacles to both share in and eventually contribute to the promise of America. These courageous people — young and old alike — had to leave behind family and friends, whom they would likely never see again. They had to make their way across the Atlantic Ocean and then struggle to find a place for themselves in the land of liberty. Today, Ellis Island portrays both the suffering and the exhilaration of immigrants as they first set foot in America. The exhibits illustrate how immigrants disembarked and were "processed" at this historic site. The redbrick buildings, the grounds, and the Great Hall evoke a haunting atmosphere of what once happened on this scrap of land. Ellis Island still echoes with the hopes, dreams, and fears of so many immigrants.

NATIVE AMERICANS originally referred to Ellis Island as "Kiosh," or Gull Island. Later, the Dutch and then the English called it Oyster Island because of its rich oyster beds. For nearly 150 years the little island was a popular spot for picnics, clambakes, and oyster roasts. A New Jersey farmer named Samuel Ellis then bought the island, but when he died in 1794, New York State took it for nonpayment of taxes. Because the island was ideally located for defense of the harbor, the federal government then acquired it from the State of New York. It served as a fort and munitions storage facility under various names, but again became known as Ellis Island in 1861 — long before it became the most important immigration station in America.

ABOVE: *Today, people may learn about the history of Ellis Island and immigration at various exhibits at the museum.*

FACING PAGE: *Immigrants could bring only a few belongings—only what they could carry with them.*

Prior to 1890 individual states regulated immigration to the United States. From 1855 to 1890, for example, Castle Garden, an old fort in the Battery on the lower tip of Manhattan, served as the New York State immigration station. About eight million immigrants, mostly from England, Ireland, Germany, and Scandinavian countries, entered the United States through this portal. These early immigrants constituted the first massive waves of people who settled and populated the United States. Yet throughout the nineteenth century, economic hardships, political unrest, and religious persecution in Europe continued to drive what would become the largest mass migration in human history. It soon became apparent that Castle Garden could not handle the rising tide of immigrants.

It was decided that the federal government would be best suited to oversee immigration to the United States. In 1890, President Benjamin Harrison designated Ellis Island as the site of the first Federal Immigration Station for the Port of New York. The House Committee on Immigration authorized construction of new buildings there. While the Ellis Island station was under construction, immigrants were processed at the Barge Office on the Battery on the southeast tip of Manhattan.

Over the next two years, Ellis Island was enlarged to six acres, nearly doubling in size, with landfill from the ballast of incoming steamships that brought immigrants to America and with rocks and soil from the excavation of the New York subway tunnels. Ellis Island was now large enough to accommodate several wooden buildings, notably the immigration depot, a two-story-high structure of "Georgia pine" with a slate roof. A story in *Harper's Weekly* described the station as a "latter-day watering place hotel, presenting to the view a great many-windowed expanse of buff-painted wooden walls, of blue slate roofing, and of light and picturesque towers." The most prominent feature of the main building was the registry room, measuring two hundred by one hundred feet, with an impressive fifty-six-foot vaulted ceiling. New arrivals made their way along twelve aisles, separated by iron bars, to the front of the room where doctors examined them.

Keeping the name from its earlier owner, Ellis Island formally opened on New Year's Day, 1892. Accompanied by her two brothers, Annie Moore entered the annals of history and her new country as the very first immigrant to pass through Ellis Island. The next day the *New York Times* described the grand event:

41

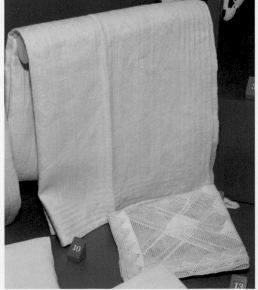

These displays show some of the cherished objects, including family heirlooms, that immigrants brought to America.

"There were three big steamships in the harbor waiting to land their passengers and there was much anxiety among the newcomers to be the first landed at the new station. The honor was reserved for a rosy-cheeked Irish girl. She was Annie Moore, fifteen years of age, lately a resident of County Cork and yesterday one of the 148 steerage passengers landing from the steamship *Nevada*.

"As soon as the gangplank was run ashore Annie tripped across it and hurried into the big building that almost covers the entire island. By a prearranged plan she was escorted to a registry desk which was temporarily occupied by Mr. Charles M. Hendley, the former private secretary of Secretary [of the Treasury William] Windom . . . When the little voyager had been registered, Col. Weber [the commissioner of immigration] presented her with a $10 gold piece and made a short address of congratulations and welcome. It was the first United States coin she had ever seen and the largest amount of money she had ever possessed."

ABOVE: *This newspaper article from 1891 portrays immigrants who came to America from many other countries.*

LEFT: *This statue portrays Annie Moore, who was the first of millions of immigrants from many countries to pass through Ellis Island.*

Over the next sixty-two years, from 1892 to 1954, more than twelve million impoverished, hungry, and oppressed men, women, and children followed in Annie's footsteps through the small gateway of Ellis Island. About three million of these newcomers were children.

Ellis Island became the most renowned port of entry in the United States. As the steamships approached the island, they passed the Statue of Liberty. At the base of this great monument is an inscription from a poem entitled "The New Colossus" by Emma Lazarus:

> Give me your tired, your poor,
> Your huddled masses yearning to breathe free,
> The wretched refuse of your teeming shore.
> Send these, the homeless, tempest-tost to me,
> I lift my lamp beside the golden door!

To most immigrants, Ellis Island did become "the golden door" into America and a better life. However, during the evening of June 14, 1897, just five years after Ellis Island had opened, a fire of unknown origin, possibly faulty wiring, broke out. It burned the Georgia-pine buildings, including the main depot, to the ground. No one died in the fire, but priceless federal and state immigration records dating back to 1855 were destroyed.

ABOVE: *With red-brick walls and white limestone trim, the main building at Ellis Island still looks much as it did in 1892.*

FACING PAGE: *The Statue of Liberty was one of the first sights in New York Harbor for millions of immigrants arriving on steamships.*

The United States Treasury promptly ordered the immigration station to be rebuilt with one condition — all future structures on Ellis Island had to be fireproof. Over the next two years, while a new immigration station was being built on Ellis Island, immigrants were again processed at the Barge Office. On December 17, 1900, the new main building, which was constructed of red brick trimmed with limestone in a French Renaissance architectural style, was opened and 2,251 immigrants passed through that day.

Ellis Island once again welcomed millions of people who sailed into New York Harbor for their first glimpse of the United States. Edward Corsi, who at age ten came to America with his family from Italy in 1907, later wrote, "My first impression of the new world will always remain etched in my memory, particularly that hazy October morning when I first saw Ellis Island.

"The steamer *Florida*, fourteen days out of Naples, filled to capacity with 1,600 natives of Italy, had weathered one of the worst storms in our captain's memory . . . My mother, my stepfather, my brother Giuseppe, and my two sisters, Liberta and Helvetia, all of us together, happy that we had come through the storm safely, clustered on the foredeck for fear of separation and looked with wonder on this miraculous land of our dreams.

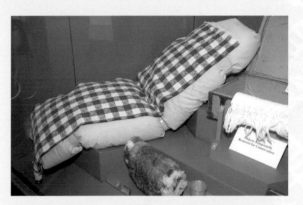

ABOVE: *An immigrant child slept on this small mattress in the steerage section during the long journey across the Atlantic Ocean.*

FACING PAGE: *This photo on display at Ellis Island shows how steerage passengers crowded into the lower level of a steamship.*

"Passengers all about us were crowding against the rail. Jabbered conversation, sharp cries, laughs, and cheers — a steady rising din filled the air. Mothers and fathers lifted up the babies so that they too could see, off to the left, the Statue of Liberty . . . looming shadowy through the mist, it brought silence to the decks of the *Florida.*

"The symbol of America, this enormous expression of what we had all been taught was the inner meaning of this new country we were coming to — inspired awe in the hopeful immigrants."

Steamships brought European immigrants to many American ports, including

Boston, Philadelphia, Baltimore, Savannah, Miami, and New Orleans. Asian immigrants, most from China, came through Angel Island near San Francisco. However, most European immigrants entered the United States through Ellis Island, which was the most popular destination of steamship companies. Over these immigration years, the steamships for companies like White Star, Red Star, Cunard, and Hamburg-America carried millions of immigrants to Ellis Island and other ports of entry into the United States.

Yet it was hard, often painful, to leave one's family and board these steamships. Italian immigrant Luciano De-Crescenzo recalled, "Many immigrants had brought onboard balls of yarn, leaving one end of the line with someone on land. As the ship slowly cleared the dock, the balls unwound amid the farewell shouts of the women, the fluttering of handkerchief, and the infants held high. After the yarn ran out, the

ABOVE: *With ferryboats lined up at the dock, this was a rush day at Ellis Island, which was always a very busy place.*

RIGHT: *In this poster, a man waves his hat in homage to the Statue of Liberty, which welcomed so many immigrants as they sailed into New York Harbor.*

FACING PAGE: *Immigrants often arrived at Ellis Island weary and homesick for family and friends left behind in the "Old Country" in Europe.*

long strips remained airborne, sustained by the wind, long after those on land and those at sea had lost sight of each other."

Most of these friends and family knew that they were saying goodbye forever. A Russian teenager remembered leaving his parents at the railroad station in a small town: "When the train drew into the station my mother lost control of her feelings.

As she embraced me for the last time her sobs became violent and Father had to separate us. There was despair in her way of clinging to me, which I could not understand then. I understand it now. I never saw her again."

An overwhelming number of passengers — about nine out of every ten immigrants arriving at Ellis Island — made the sea voyage in third class, or steerage. Even then, they could barely afford a ticket, which cost between ten and fifteen dollars. So immigrants often had to borrow money from relatives already in America or sell much of what they owned to purchase a ticket. These third-class or "steerage" immigrants faced many hardships during their journey of about two weeks. A thousand people sometimes crowded into the damp and dirty bottom level of a large steamship. These immigrants had little food and few, if any, comforts. There was no fresh air and little light. Only during fair weather were people allowed to go to the upper deck. They often languished seasick in their bunks during rough, two-week crossings of the Atlantic Ocean. So many steerage passengers, mostly children and the elderly, died aboard from typhus, fever, and other diseases that newspapers referred to the vessels as "coffin ships" or "swimming coffins."

When they finally arrived in New York Harbor, steamships docked at piers on the Hudson or East River. Wealthy passengers who traveled first class and second class usually did not

LEFT AND ABOVE: *Immigrant children had to bring all of their possessions with them—a girl's doll and a boy's pair of shoes are now displayed at Ellis Island.*

FACING PAGE: *Suitcases and trunks of all immigrants were piled high in the baggage room on the main floor at Ellis Island.*

have to undergo an inspection process at Ellis Island. It was assumed that anyone who had enough money to purchase an expensive steamship ticket could afford to live in the United States and would not become a burden on society. Only those who appeared to be sick or to have legal problems were sent to Ellis Island for further inspection. These first-class immigrants underwent a quick inspection while still onboard the ship, disembarked, passed through customs at the docks, and then freely entered the United States.

However, all the steerage passengers had to pass through Ellis Island. Transported from the ship by ferry or barge to Ellis Island, every one of these arrivals had to undergo a thorough inspection of their fitness to become citizens of the

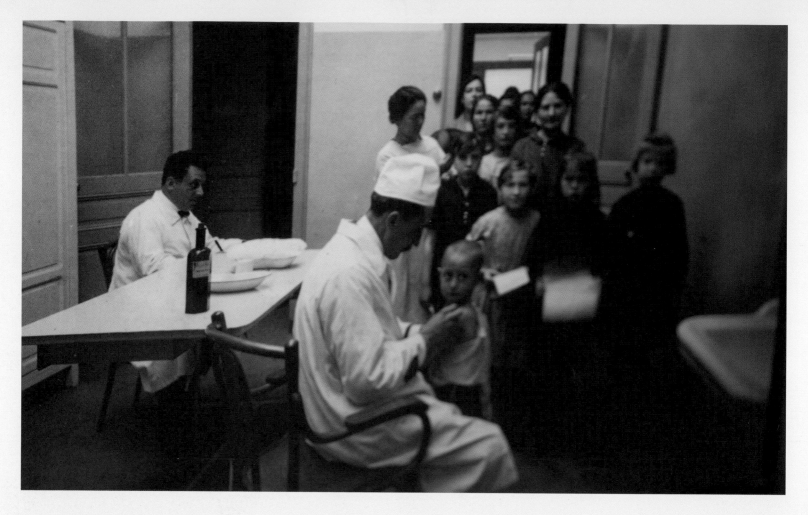

RIGHT: *Immigrant children being examined by doctors at Ellis Island before they were allowed to enter the United States.*

FACING PAGE: *Slavic immigrants jammed the stairs at Ellis Island, carrying their most precious belongings with them.*

United States. From the docks at Ellis Island, the immigrants carted their heavy trunks and suitcases inside to the baggage room of the main building. This luggage held nearly all that the immigrants owned: clothing, household goods, and personal belongings. Many people were afraid to leave their trunks there because they might be lost or stolen. "When we got to Ellis Island," recalled English immigrant Eleanor Lenhart, "they put the gangplank down and there was a man on foot, and he was shouting at the top of his voice, 'Put your luggage here, drop your luggage here. Men this way. Women and children this way.' Dad looked at us and said, 'We'll meet you back here at this mound of luggage and hope we find it and you again and see you later.' "

From the baggage room, immigrants made their way up a flight of stairs to the second floor, lugging small bags and bundles of the most precious of their belongings. They weren't aware of it, but their medical examinations had already begun. Doctors carefully observed immigrants from the tops of the stairs for signs of any health problems. They made a chalk mark on the shoulder of any immigrant with a suspected malady. There were more than a dozen letters for various ailments: H for heart, L for lameness, and X for mental illness.

If a chalk mark was made, doctors then briefly inspected an immigrant for physical ailments. Doctors at Ellis

REGISTRY DEPARTMENT, ELLIS ISLAND. *C&H Feb 1898*

ABOVE: *Immigrants stood before inspectors seated at high desks and answered a series of questions before being allowed into the country.*

FACING PAGE: *Immigrants slowly made their way along the rows called "pens" on their way to inspections before entry into the United States.*

FOLLOWING SPREAD: *Today, the registry room at Ellis Island echoes with the memories of the millions of immigrants who passed through here.*

Island became very adept at conducting what came to be known as "six-second physicals." By 1916, some people joked that a doctor could identify a variety of medical conditions by simply glancing at an immigrant. At that time, there were about fifty medical reasons for deporting any immigrant. Helen Barth, a volunteer for the Hebrew Immigrant Aid Society from 1914 to 1917, recalled, "The doctor would have them put their hands down on the desk and if [their fingernails] showed pink, he passed them as not suffering from a heart condition. But when the nails were very blue he was put aside as a heart case."

Immigrants came to dread the painful "buttonhook test" for a contagious disease of the eyes known as trachoma. In 1897, the U.S. Surgeon General declared that trachoma was a serious disease and the following year doctors at Ellis Island examined all immigrants with red, watery, or inflamed eyes. Beginning in 1905, all immigrants arriving at Ellis Island were examined for trachoma during line inspection. In this examination, inspectors turned the eyelids inside out with a buttonhook, a tool normally used to loop buttons on shoes. Trachoma became one of the most prevalent reasons for refusing entry into the United States.

After the immigrants had gone through a medical examination, they were herded into the registry room, or Great Hall, where inspections took place. This huge space was divided by iron rails and wire rows that resembled cattle pens, until 1911, when long, wooden benches replaced these fences. Yugoslavian immigrant Ljubica Wuchina called it "The big room packed with people, surging with people." The immigrants slowly made their way along winding rows to the west end, where they underwent a lengthy interview. Here, inspectors sat behind tall desks with interpreters nearby. Describing the rush periods at Ellis Island, one overworked inspector said, "We were swamped by that human tide."

Immigrants came forward in groups of thirty, matching the number on each page of the ship's manifest log. All immigrants had papers issued at the port of departure that included their names, the name of their ship, and the page of the manifest log on which they were listed. Inspectors first reviewed this manifest log, which had been filled out at the port of embarkation in Europe. The inspectors then asked twenty-nine questions of each immigrant, including name, age, and occupation. They also wanted to know the amount of money that immigrants had, if they were married, and if anyone was waiting for them. Inspectors at Ellis Island used this document to cross-examine every steerage passenger. The newcomers were supposed to have some money with them, about twenty-five dollars, which was a huge sum for an impoverished person. Those who didn't have enough money might be detained until friends or relatives sent money to them at the island—or could be sent back to their home country. Armenian immigrant Albert Mardirossian reminisced, "Ellis Island—you got thousands of people marching in, a little bit excited, a little bit scared. Just imagine you're fourteen and a half years old and you're in a strange country and you don't know what's going to happen."

The noted photographer Lewis Hine captured this picture of beleaguered Italian immigrants searching for their lost baggage.

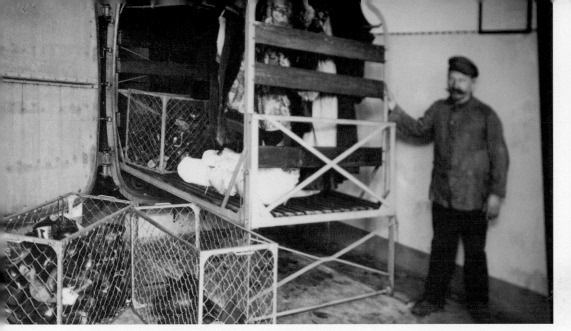

Edward Ferro, an inspector at Ellis Island, who himself had emigrated from Italy in 1906 at age twelve, explained, "The language was a problem of course, but it was overcome by the use of interpreters. We had interpreters on the island who spoke practically every language.

"It would happen sometimes that these interpreters—some of them—were really softhearted people and hated to see people being deported, and they would, at times, help the aliens by interpreting in such a manner as to benefit the alien and not the government.

"Unless you saw it, you couldn't visualize the misery of these people who came to the United States from Europe . . . They were tired; they had gone through an awful lot of hardships. It's impossible for anyone who had not gone through the experience to imagine what it was."

If the immigrants were in good health and if their papers were in order, the Ellis Island inspection process lasted from three to five hours and the immigrants were

Detained immigrants had to stay on Ellis Island until it was decided if they could enter the country or would be deported. They had to wash up at sinks and sleep in narrow bunks, which are today displayed in the museum at Ellis Island.

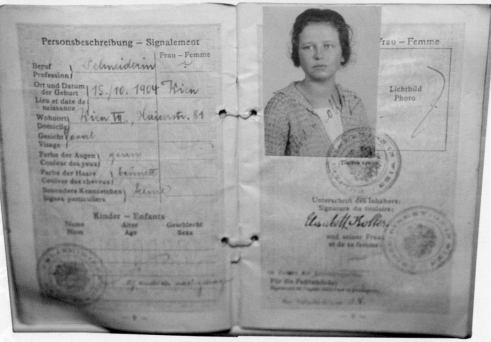

approved. Immigrants then descended the Staircase of Separation at the end of the Great Hall. A turn to the left led to the dock and a short ferry ride to Manhattan. However, many immigrants ended up being held on the small island. When these people reached the foot of the stairs, they had to go straight ahead to the detention rooms.

Most immigrants were briefly delayed for questioning, then allowed to continue on their way. Writer Louis Adamic, who came from Slovenia, a small country in southeastern Europe, described the night he spent on Ellis Island after coming to America in 1913. He lay on one of many bunk beds among other immigrants in a huge hall. Lacking even a blanket, the young man recalled that he "shivered, sleepless, all night, listening to snores" and dreams "in perhaps a dozen different languages."

Others could be detained longer for several reasons: political views, criminal history, or inability to support themselves. Some immigrants would be marked with a chalk "SI," which meant Special Inquiry. These detainees had to live in crowded dormitories, or they might be confined to the hospital on Ellis Island. Those with a medical condition had to be hospitalized for days or weeks until they recovered from an illness.

Many of these detainees were eventually allowed to enter the country, but more than three thousand immigrants died in the hospital buildings on Ellis Island and many people were deported. "The place was filled . . . There were [people] who had been there for weeks and some for months, some as much as a year," remembered Yugoslavian detainee Paul Laric. "And there was a feeling of desperation because we had no idea when we would get out and neither did other people."

Those who failed to meet the medical, economic, or legal requirements for entry into the United States were sent back to Europe. Some immigrants were not allowed into the country, because they were criminals or anarchists who sought to overthrow the U.S. government. However, most immigrants were denied entry if a doctor determined that they had a contagious disease that would endanger the public safety or if a legal inspector thought they were so poor and unskilled that they would be "likely to become a public charge."

Immigrants most dreaded the possibility of deportation, which was a devastating fate for them. Having sold everything, many deportees had no home to which they could return in the "old country." Recalling those who were sent back, Ellis Island Commissioner Henry H. Curran wrote, "I was powerless. I could only watch them go. Day by day the [ferries] took them from Ellis Island back to the ships again, back to the ocean, back to what?"

After 1917, immigrants had to hold passports from their home countries when they arrived at Ellis Island and entered the United States.

One of the most famous photographs of immigration is Alfred Stieglitz's *The Steerage* (1907). This image portrays the sharp contrast between the wealthy, or "the mob called the 'rich,'" as Stieglitz referred to the wealthy people, and the impoverished crowded onto the lower deck of a steamship. Stieglitz explained, "There were men, women and children on the lower level of the steerage . . . The scene fascinated me: A round straw hat; the funnel leaning left, the stairway leaning right; the white drawbridge, its railings made of chain; white suspenders crossed on the back of a man below; circular iron machinery; a mast that cut into the sky, completing a triangle. I stood spellbound for a while. I saw shapes related to one another—a picture of shapes, and underlying it, a new vision that held me."

However, this steamship was *not* bringing immigrants to America. It was heading east—returning people to their home countries in Europe. Inspectors deported about two percent of all immigrants, but twelve million people arrived at Ellis Island. So, many

thousands of immigrants were forced to make the long, hard journey back to Europe. Frederick Wallis, commissioner of Ellis Island for a little more than a year in 1920 and 1921, said, "I do believe that our nation is committing a gross injustice for which some day it must render an account, in allowing these hundreds of thousands of people to sell all they have, sever all connections, come four thousand miles out of the heart of Europe and other countries, only to find after passing the Statue of Liberty that they must go back to the country whence they came." In leaving office, he recommended that the inspection process be transferred from Ellis Island to American consulates overseas, so that prospective immigrants would not have to make the heartbreaking journey back across the ocean. His suggestions were eventually adopted, but not until decades later.

ABOVE LEFT AND RIGHT: *Immigrants detained on Ellis Island generally received good food in the dining hall, along with shelter and health care.*

FACING PAGE: *One of the most famous immigration photographs,* The Steerage, *actually shows immigrants returning to Europe.*

Over the years, Ellis Island came to be known as "the island of hope, the island of tears" because of the many inspiring stories and tragic events that occurred there. For most immigrants, it was a place of great joy—ranging from the simple pleasure of tasting a new food to life-changing experiences. Maljan Chavoor recalled the day he arrived at Ellis Island as a boy and enjoyed a special dessert that was served in the dining room there: "Jell-O. I fell in love with it. The first time in my life I had Jell-O. I've been eating Jell-O for seventy years since I've been here."

Ellis Island also became the site of reunions of families and friends who hadn't

ABOVE: *After passing through Ellis Island, immigrants such as this group of Italians waited to be transported into New York City.*

FACING PAGE: *Immigrant children detained on Ellis Island enjoyed the outdoor playground with the New York City skyline in the background.*

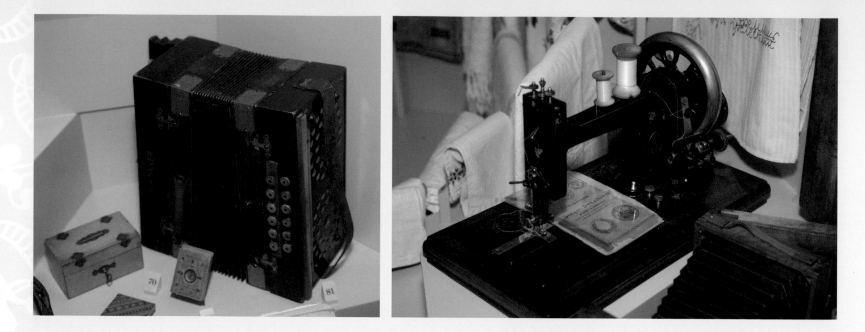

ABOVE LEFT AND RIGHT: *The Ellis Island Museum now displays some of the cherished belongings that immigrants carried with them to America.*

seen each other for years. Many immigrants fell in love and married on the little island. Frank Martocci, who emigrated from Italy, arriving at Ellis Island in 1897 at age thirty, later became an inspector at the famed port of entry. He recalled, "It seems to me now, as I look back, that in those days there were crying and laughing and singing all the time at Ellis Island. Very often brides came over to marry here, and of course we had to act as witnesses. I have no count, but I'm sure I must have helped at hundreds and hundreds of weddings of all nationalities and all types.

"There is a post at Ellis Island which through long usage had come to earn the name of 'the Kissing Post.' It was probably the spot of greatest interest on the island, and if the immigrants recall it afterwards it is always, I am sure, with fondness. For myself, I found it a real joy to watch some of the tender scenes that took place there . . . where friends, sweethearts, husbands and wives, parents and children would embrace and kiss and shed tears for pure joy."

After making their way through Ellis Island, most immigrants worked hard and eventually prospered in the United States of America.

Ellis Island was indeed "the golden door" for most immigrants, who soon made their way into the bustling city of New York with hope in their hearts. As one Slovenian arrival reflected, "The city dazzled us. We had never seen such buildings, such people, such activity. Maybe the stories were true. Maybe everything was possible in America."

Of course, most immigrants realized that they faced many challenges and that they would have to work hard in achieving the American dream. Italian immigrants joked among themselves, "I came to America because I heard the streets

were lined with gold. When I got here, I found out three things: First the streets weren't paved with gold; second, they weren't paved at all; and third, I was expected to pave them."

Yet most immigrants went on to great success in their new home. Among the immigrants who passed through Ellis Island and eventually became famous were Irving Berlin, Frank Capra, Claudette Colbert, Max Ernst, Max Factor, Felix Frankfurter, Marcus Garvey, Bob Hope, Al Jolson, Bela Lugosi, Ayn Rand, James Reston, Knute Rockne, Arthur Rubinstein, Ben Shahn, and many others.

Golda Meir, who later became a distinguished prime minister of Israel, emigrated from Russia and arrived at Ellis Island in 1906, at age eight. She recalled, "My father, who had by now moved from New York to Milwaukee, was barely making a living. He wrote back that he hoped to get a job working on the railway and soon he would have enough money for our tickets . . . I can remember only the hustle and bustle of those last weeks in Pinsk, the farewells from the family, the embraces and the tears. Going to America then was almost like going to the moon . . . We were bound

Over the years, Ellis Island continually expanded, but the main building of red bricks and limestone trim always dominated the grounds.

LOOKING BACKWARD.

for places about which we knew nothing at all and for a country that was totally strange to us."

During the early 1900s, federal officials mistakenly speculated that the era of mass immigration had already peaked. In reality, millions of people longed to come to America. In 1907 more immigrants poured into the United States than in any other year, more than one million of them passing through Ellis Island. The peak day of that year was April 17, when 11,747 immigrants went through a station designed to handle 5,000 people a day.

Over the years, the Ellis Island grounds were gradually enlarged to twenty-seven and a half acres. Carpenters and masons labored continually to expand buildings and construct new facilities to handle these waves of immigrants. Between 1900 and 1915, they built dormitories, kitchens, hospitals, and contagious-disease wards.

When the United States entered World War I, immigration sharply decreased. Officials brought many suspected enemy aliens from throughout the country to Ellis Island. These detained aliens were then moved to other locations so that the United States Navy and Army Medical

THE AMERICANESE WALL, AS CONGRESSMAN BURNETT WOULD BUILD IT.

UNCLE SAM: You're welcome in — if you can climb it!

ABOVE LEFT AND RIGHT: *Under pressure from nativists, the United States government passed laws, such as a literacy test, to restrict immigration.*

FACING PAGE: *Although their ancestors had been immigrants, many Americans came to oppose further immigration, especially from eastern and southern Europe, as depicted in these political cartoons.*

Department could utilize Ellis Island for the rest of the war. During this time, immigrants were inspected on board ship or at the docks. After the Russian Revolution of 1917 and the Communist takeover of that nation, the "Red Scare" swept across the United States and thousands of suspected alien revolutionaries were held at Ellis Island. Hundreds of these people were later deported simply because they were suspected of associating with radical groups. In 1920, Ellis Island opened again as an immigration station and 225,206 newcomers passed through the facility that year.

From the beginning of the mass immigration in 1880, many people known as "nativists" opposed immigration. They wanted to limit the composition of the country to "old immigrants" from northern and western Europe. They believed that people from southern and eastern Europe were inferior to the earlier immigrants

and demanded restrictions on entering the United States. They lobbied the U.S. government, which passed laws, such as the Chinese Exclusion Act and the Alien Contract Labor Law, and then a literacy test, in an effort to stop immigration. However, these restrictions could not slow the flood of immigrants. The first serious limitation at Ellis Island and other immigration stations began in 1921 with the passage of the "Quota Laws" and the National Origins Act in 1924. These laws restricted the immigration of ethnic groups to certain percentages, taking into account those already living in the United States according to the censuses of 1890 and 1910.

Following World War I, the United States was also emerging as an international power and opening embassies throughout the world. Immigrants began to apply for visas at these consulates in their countries of origin. Anyone wishing to come to America completed paperwork and underwent medical examinations there. From

then until it closed in 1954, Ellis Island was no longer needed as an immigration station. It became primarily a facility for detainees. During World War II, Japanese, Italian, and German people were held on the island—both aliens and citizens—totaling seven thousand by 1946. Most of these detainees were German Americans

This architectural rendering offers a broad, elevated view of the renovations envisioned for Ellis Island.

who had been wrongly accused of being Nazis. The United States Coast Guard also trained about sixty thousand men there. In November 1954, Arne Peterssen, a Norwegian merchant seaman who was the last detainee, was released, and Ellis Island officially closed.

Despite the obstacles that had restricted immigration for many years, the 1953 report of the Commission on Immigration and Naturalization appointed by President Harry S. Truman stated, "Our growth as a nation has been achieved in large measure, through the genius and industry of immigrants of every race and from every quarter of the world. The story of their pursuit of happiness is the saga of America."

In 1965, President Lyndon B. Johnson designated Ellis Island as part of the Statue of Liberty National Monument. From 1976 to 1984 the famous immigration station was opened to the public on a limited basis. Beginning in 1984, Ellis Island underwent a major renovation—the largest historic restoration in American history. The $160 million project was funded by many donations to the Statue of Liberty–Ellis Island Foundation and the National Park Service. More than twenty million Americans contributed to the restoration. On September 10, 1990, the main building opened to the public as the Ellis Island Immigration Museum. Nearly two million people now visit Ellis Island every year.

The United States Public Health Service and the Bureau of

Many areas of Ellis Island have not yet been renovated and opened to the general public.

ABOVE: *Like their ancestors who took ferries from their steamships to Ellis Island, visitors now ride the ferry from Battery Park to the famous landmark.*

FACING PAGE: *With lights shining brightly, a ferryboat pulls away from Ellis Island, which is silhouetted against the night sky.*

Immigration, which later became the Immigration and Naturalization Service (INS), were responsible for "processing" immigrants at Ellis Island. However, on March 1, 2003, the Immigration and Naturalization Service was reorganized and became part of the U.S. Department of Homeland Security, thereby marking a new era in the history of American immigration. Today, Ellis Island stands as a remarkable monument to this fascinating chapter in the history of the United States. Since its restoration and opening as a museum in 1990, tens of millions of people have taken the ferry ride to Ellis Island to walk in the footsteps of their ancestors.

Further Reading

The following books were consulted in the preparation of *Ellis Island: Coming to the Land of Liberty*. Many of the quotes in the book were drawn from the Ellis Island Oral History Project.

Amore, B. *An Italian American Odyssey: Life Line — Filo Della Vita: Through Ellis Island and Beyond*. New York: Center for Migration Studies, 2006.

Bell, James B., and Richard I. Abrams. *In Search of Liberty: The Story of the Statue of Liberty and Ellis Island*. Garden City, N.Y.: Doubleday, 1984.

Benton, Barbara. *Ellis Island: A Pictorial History*. New York: Facts on File Publications, 1987.

Brownstone, David M., Irene M. Franck, and Douglass L. Brownstone. *Island of Hope, Island of Tears*. New York: Barnes & Noble Books, 2000.

Burdick, John. *Ellis Island: Gateway of Hope*. New York: Smithmark Books, 1997.

Coan, Peter M. *Ellis Island Interviews: Immigrants Tell Their Stories in Their Own Words*. New York: Barnes & Noble Books, 2004.

Conway, Lorie. *Forgotten Ellis Island: The Extraordinary Story of America's Immigrant Hospital*. New York: Smithsonian Books–Collins, 2007.

Corsi, Edward. *In the Shadow of Liberty*. New York: Arno Press, 1969.

Davies, Nancy Millichap. *Gateway to America: Liberty Island and Ellis Island*. New York: Smithmark Books, 1992.

Kotker, Norman, and Susan Jonas. *Ellis Island: Echoes from a Nation's Past*. New York: Aperture Foundation, 1989.

FACING PAGE: *As they passed through Ellis Island, some immigrants hastily scratched graffiti onto the walls of the Great Hall. Written in fourteen different languages, the scribbles and drawings were perhaps left as a remembrance for future generations.*

Moreno, Barry. *Encyclopedia of Ellis Island*. Westport, Conn.: Greenwood Press, 2004.

Reeves, Pamela. *Ellis Island: Gateway to the American Dream*. New York: Barnes & Noble Books, 2002.

Shapiro, Mary J. *Gateway to Liberty: The Story of the Statue of Liberty and Ellis Island*. New York: Vintage Books, 1986.

Sherman, Augustus F., and Peter Mesenhöller. *Augustus F. Sherman: Ellis Island Portraits, 1905–1920*. New York: Aperture Foundation, 2005.

Statue of Liberty, Ellis Island Immigration Museum: Statue of Liberty National Monument, New Jersey/New York. Washington, D.C.: National Park Service, U.S. Dept. of the Interior, 1999.

Tifft, Wilton S. *Ellis Island*. Chicago: Contemporary Books, 1990.

*When they came to the United States, immigrants tried to bring along at least a few cherished objects that reflected their rich heritage, such as beautifully designed books in their native language (*FACING PAGE*) or intricately embroidered and decorated clothing (*ABOVE*).*

Children's Books

Hicks, Terry Allan. *Ellis Island*. New York: Marshall Cavendish Benchmark, 2007.

Houghton, Gillian. *Ellis Island: A Primary Source History of an Immigrant's Arrival in America*. New York: Rosen Pub. Group, 2004.

Knowlton, Mary Lee, and Dale Anderson. *Arriving at Ellis Island*. Milwaukee, Wis.: Gareth Stevens Pub., 2002.

Kroll, Steven, and Karen Ritz. *Ellis Island: Doorway to Freedom*. New York: Holiday House, 1995.

Lawlor, Veronica. *I Was Dreaming to Come to America: Memories from the Ellis Island Oral History Project*. New York: Viking, 1995.

Marcovitz, Hal. *Ellis Island*. Philadelphia: Mason Crest Publishers, 2003.

Rebman, Renee C. *Life on Ellis Island*. San Diego, Calif.: Lucent Books, 2000.

Sandler, Martin W. *Island of Hope: The Story of Ellis Island and the Journey to America*. New York: Scholastic, 2004.